Copyrigh

Legal & Disclaimer

The information contained in this book and its contents is not designed to replace or take the place of any form of medical or professional advice; and is not meant to replace the need for independent medical, financial, legal or other professional advice or services, as may be required. The content and information in this book have been provided for educational and entertainment purposes only.

You agree that by continuing to read this book, where appropriate and/or necessary, you shall consult a professional (including but not limited to your doctor, attorney, or financial advisor or such other advisor as needed) before using any of the suggested remedies, techniques, or information in this book.

TABLE OF CONTENTS

INTRODUCTION

Good nutrition is a must for keeping COPD in check. But the shortness of breath that often accompanies COPD can sometimes interfere with your body's ability to get the right nutrients. COPD is the fourth-leading cause of death in the United States, preceded by heart disease, cancer, and accidents. It affects more than 8 million Americans and predominantly occurs in people who are middle-aged or older. However, millions of adults have evidence of impaired lung function, indicating that there is a high probability of underdiagnosis.

In this book, you'll discover the realities and challenges of the condition, but also the best treatments, helpful lifestyle changes to help you manage the condition as well as easy and delicious recipes to help relieve your symptoms.

SECTION ONE: COPD BASICS

What Is Chronic Obstructive Pulmonary Disease (Copd)

Chronic obstructive pulmonary disease (COPD) is a progressive, irreversible inflammatory disease of the lungs that makes it hard to breathe. Common symptoms include a persistent cough, wheezing, production of phlegm, shortness of breath, and a feeling of tightness in your chest, though these symptoms may not be noticeable until you're in the later stages of the disease.

COPD is not curable, but it's a preventable and treatable illness. The earlier you start treatment, the better your prognosis.

Effect on the Lungs

COPD is characterized by lung obstruction and a limitation of airflow in the lungs. It is associated with an abnormal inflammatory response of your lungs to noxious stimuli, like cigarette smoke, air pollution, or harsh chemicals.

In COPD, airflow is diminished due to one or more of the following factors:

• The bronchi (air tubes) and alveoli (air sacs where gas exchange takes place) lose their elasticity and are unable to adequately stretch open when you inhale (breath in).

• The walls that lie between the alveoli get destroyed, causing enlarged spaces throughout the lungs.

• The lining of the air tubes becomes thick and inflamed.

• The air tubes secrete more mucus than they should, causing them to clog.

Airflow limitation in COPD generally worsens unless the risk factors (such as smoking) are discontinued. Even then, it is not fully reversible.

Types of Chronic Obstructive Pulmonary Disease

COPD is actually an umbrella term that's used to describe a group of obstructive lung diseases including:

• Emphysema: A disease that results from damage to the alveoli, emphysema is most often caused by smoking. Fewer alveoli are available for oxygen exchange because they become destroyed by inflammation and scarring. The remaining alveoli lose their elasticity, which causes them to trap air with each exhalation. This is similar to a latex balloon that has lost its elasticity and traps air as it collapses.

• Chronic bronchitis: With chronic bronchitis, your airways become chronically inflamed, resulting in scarring and thickening. This process also frequently causes an increased production of mucus, which then fills the airways, further obstructing your breathing.

• Bronchiectasis: In bronchiectasis, your airways are dilated (widened), often as a result of recurrent respiratory infections during your childhood. The inflammation also increases the production of mucus, further clogging your airways.

Quite often, people with COPD have a combination of these disorders at the same time. It's also possible to have an asthma component with the disease, which is an important factor when considering treatment.

Chronic Obstructive Pulmonary Disease Symptoms

COPD is often asymptomatic (without symptoms) until significant damage to the lungs has already occurred. It's a progressive disease characterized by stretches of relative stability, alternating with intermittent exacerbations (worsening).

Common symptoms may include:

• Shortness of breath (dyspnea), especially after exertion

• Persistent, daily cough

• Sputum production (coughing up phlegm) which can be clear, white, yellow, or green in color

• Wheezing

• Fatigue

• Frequent lung infections

• Chest tightness

• Cyanosis (a bluish discoloration of the lips and nail beds)

Additional signs and symptoms that may accompany the more severe stages of the disease include weight loss, loss of appetite (anorexia), and fatigue.

Ankle, foot, or leg swelling may occur as a result of medication side effects or due to co-existing heart problems.

Anxiety and depression are common emotional symptoms of COPD. Treatment aimed at managing mood may be necessary to improve your quality of life and lower your risk of COPD exacerbation.

Causes

Some causes of COPD include exposure to cigarette smoking (whether you smoke yourself or have been exposed to secondhand smoke); occupational exposure to chemicals; indoor and outdoor air pollution; and, far less often, a genetic disorder called alpha-1-antitrypsin (AAT) deficiency.

Asthma is also a risk factor for COPD.

Diagnosis

To make an accurate diagnosis of chronic obstructive pulmonary disease, a complete history and physical assessment must be taken. It should start with your healthcare provider asking you questions about your family history, as well as your history of exposure to tobacco smoke and other types of environmental and/or occupational exposures.

Diagnostic tests may include:

• Blood tests, including arterial blood gases, which can assess your blood oxygen levels

• Chest X-ray, which can show signs of COPD

• Pulmonary function tests, such as spirometry, lung diffusion tests, or body plethysmography, to assess your inspiratory and expiratory capabilities

• Pulse oximetry, a non-invasive measure of blood oxygen that is less precise than arterial blood gas

• Screening for AAT deficiency to identify the rare genetic cause of COPD

There are four stages of COPD: mild, moderate, severe, and very severe. Staging is generally diagnosed in your doctor's office with a spirometry test.

Treatment

With proper treatment, COPD can be controlled. That said, there are factors that influence COPD life expectancy, especially the degree of airway obstruction, the severity of your dyspnea, your exercise tolerance, and your body mass index (BMI).

The best treatment for COPD if you're a smoker is to quit as soon as possible. While this won't reverse the damage you already have, it can help slow the progression of your disease.

Other treatment options include:

• Medications: Common COPD medications include inhaled bronchodilators, inhaled corticosteroids, oral steroids, expectorants, phosphodiesterase-4 inhibitors, and antibiotics. Treatment is often broken down into two categories: maintenance medications, which are used daily and continuously whether or not symptoms are present; and rescue medications, which are used when symptoms worsen, such as during exacerbations.

• Airway clearance techniques: These are techniques to clear mucus from your airway, including controlled coughing and chest physiotherapy. Other pulmonary hygiene techniques may also be suggested.

• Pulmonary rehabilitation: Pulmonary rehabilitation involves working with a therapist to optimize control of your breathing and coughing. Pulmonary exercises can increase your ability to tolerate physical activity without becoming short of breath.

• Oxygen therapy: When symptoms become more severe, supplemental oxygen therapy may be needed. There are many lightweight portable oxygen units that allow people with COPD to live relatively active lives.

• Lung surgery: Three forms of surgery are typically considered for the treatment of highly advanced COPD: Volume reduction surgery may be used to remove damaged lung tissue. Alternatively, your doctor may recommend a bullectomy, which is the removal of enlarged bullae in your lungs. In very severe COPD, lung transplantation may be recommended

Only a small percentage of those living with COPD qualify for surgical intervention. While COPD surgery can sometimes improve quality of life, it may not prolong survival, and these major surgical procedures entail a challenging recovery period.

SECTION TWO: NUTRITION AND MANAGING YOUR COPD

Why You're Having Trouble Eating

Because the stomach lies directly beneath the diaphragm, having a full stomach can make it more difficult to breathe, especially for those with COPD. Shortness of breath while eating is one of the reasons why people with COPD often suffer from malnutrition, a common complication of COPD.

Eat Healthy With the Basic Food Groups

Like anyone else, people with COPD can benefit from a balanced diet that includes foods from all of the basic food groups. If possible, be sure to include the following in your daily diet:

• Protein helps to build muscle mass and maintain growth and repair of cells and tissues. Foods from this group include meats, soy products, nuts, seeds, and legumes, like black beans or lentils.

• Dairy products such as milk, cheese, cream, and yogurt are rich in calcium to keep bones and teeth strong and healthy. They are a good source of protein too.

• Fruits and vegetables are filled with vitamins and minerals that our bodies need to maintain wellness. Eating five servings of fruits and vegetables a day is recommended for optimal health and disease prevention.

• Breads and starches contain complex carbohydrates that help our bodies sustain energy. Whole grains such as brown rice, whole wheat bread, oatmeal, or grits are also high in fiber.

• Fats are a necessary part of any healthy diet when used in moderation). Monounsaturated fats, such as extra virgin olive oil and canola oil, and polyunsaturated fats, such as corn and sunflower oil, are better for you than saturated fats, which are found in lard, hard margarine, cheese, bakery goods, and animal meats.

• Water helps keep you hydrated and assist in thinning out mucus. Drink eight, eight-ounce glasses of water a day, unless your doctor tells you otherwise.

Additionally, learn about COPD super foods and include them on your shopping list for maximum health benefit.

Vitamins and Other Supplements

In a perfect world, we would get all the vitamins and minerals we need from the foods we eat. When your diet is somehow lacking in nutrients, however, this isn't possible. If you have COPD, taking a multivitamin every day may be recommended to help you get the nutrients that you aren't getting from your diet. And, because COPD sometimes leaves you feeling too tired to eat, drinking a meal supplement can support your nutritional status without causing you to feel too full.

Why Your Weight Is Important

When you are underweight, your energy level can suffer dramatically. This can make it more difficult to complete activities of daily living and leave you more susceptible to infection and COPD exacerbation. On the contrary, being overweight can also negatively impact COPD, as it can increase your shortness of breath and lead to obesity. The best thing for anyone who has COPD is to maintain a healthy body weight, which can be determined by your doctor. Weighing yourself on a regular basis can help you accomplish this. Try these tips for weighing yourself:

- Weigh yourself at the same time every morning before eating and after using the bathroom. Try to wear the same weight clothing each time you weigh yourself, or step on the scale before getting dressed.
- Keep track of your weight on a separate piece of paper that is kept on the wall or near the scale. Doing this can help you see possible fluctuations in your weight over time.
- Call your doctor if you notice that you are either steadily losing weight without trying to do so, or if you gain three to five pounds in one week or less.

By following these tips, you can get the proper nutrition you need to keep COPD exacerbations at bay.

How Does Food Relate to Breathing?

The process of changing food to fuel in the body is called metabolism. Oxygen and food are the raw materials of the process, and energy and carbon dioxide are the finished products. Carbon dioxide is a waste product that we exhale.

The right mix of nutrients in your diet can help you breathe easier.

Metabolism of carbohydrates produces the most carbon dioxide for the amount of oxygen used; metabolism of fat produces the least. For some people with COPD, eating a diet with fewer carbohydrates and more fat helps them breathe easier.

The right mix of nutrients in your diet can help you breathe easier.

Nutritional Guidelines

Choose complex carbohydrates, such as whole-grain bread and pasta, fresh fruits and vegetables.

• To lose weight: Opt for fresh fruits and veggies over bread and pasta for the majority of your complex carbohydrates.

• To gain weight: Eat a variety of whole-grain carbohydrates and fresh fruits and vegetables.

Limit simple carbohydrates, including table sugar, candy, cake and regular soft drinks.

Eat 20 to 30 grams of fiber each day, from items such as bread, pasta, nuts, seeds, fruits and vegetables. Eat a good source of protein at least twice a day to help maintain strong respiratory muscles. Good choices include milk, eggs, cheese, meat, fish, poultry, nuts and dried beans or peas.

• To lose weight: Choose low-fat sources of protein such as lean meats and low-fat dairy products.

• To gain weight: Choose protein with a higher fat content, such as whole milk, whole milk cheese and yogurt.

Choose mono- and poly-unsaturated fats, which do not contain cholesterol. These are fats that are often liquid at room temperature and come from plant sources, such as canola, safflower and corn oils.

• To lose weight: Limit your intake of these fats.

• To gain weight: Add these types of fats to your meals.

Limit foods that contain trans fats and saturated fat. For example, butter, lard, fat and skin from meat, hydrogenated vegetable oils, shortening, fried foods, cookies, crackers and pastries.

Note: These are general nutritional guidelines for people living with COPD. Each person's needs are different, so talk to your doctor or RDN before you make changes to your diet.

Check Your Weight

Get in the habit of weighing yourself regularly. The scale will alert you to weight loss or gain. You should see your doctor or dietitian if you continue to lose weight or if you gain weight while following the recommended diet. There are health complications that can result from being underweight or overweight. A well-nourished body is better able to handle infections. When people with COPD get an infection, it can become serious quickly and result in hospitalization. Good nutrition can help prevent that from happening. If illness does occur, a well-nourished body can respond better to treatment.

Vitamins and minerals

Many people find taking a general-purpose multivitamin helpful. Often, people with COPD take steroids. Long-term use of steroids may increase your need for calcium. Consider taking calcium supplements. Look for one that includes vitamin D. Calcium carbonate or calcium citrate are good sources of calcium. Before adding any vitamins to your daily routine, be sure to discuss with your doctor.

Sodium

Too much sodium may cause edema (swelling) that may increase blood pressure. If edema or high blood pressure are health problems for you, talk with your doctor about how much sodium you should be eating each day. Ask your RDN about the use of spices and herbs in seasoning your food and other ways you can decrease your sodium intake.

Fluids

Drinking plenty of water is important not only to keep you hydrated, but also to help keep mucus thin for easier removal. Talk with your doctor about your water intake. A good goal for many people is 6 to 8 glasses (8 fluid ounces each) daily. Don't try to drink this much fluid at once; spread it out over the entire day. Some people find it helpful to fill a water pitcher every morning with all the water they are supposed to drink in one day. They then refill their glass from that pitcher and keep track of their progress during the course of the day. Remember, any healthy caffeine-free fluid counts toward your fluid goal, and most foods contribute a substantial amount of fluid, as well.

Using medical nutritional products

You may find it difficult to meet your nutritional needs with regular foods, especially if you need a lot of calories every day. Also, if your RDN has suggested that you get more of your calories from fat—the polyunsaturated, monounsaturated, and low-cholesterol variety—you may not be able to meet this goal easily with ordinary foods. Your RDN or doctor may suggest you drink a liquid called a medical nutritional product (supplement). Some of these products can be used as a complete diet by people who can't eat ordinary foods, or they can be added to regular meals by people who can't eat enough food.

Diet Hints

• *Rest just before eating.*

• *Eat more food early in the morning if you're usually too tired to eat later in the day.*

• *Avoid foods that cause gas or bloating. They tend to make breathing more difficult.*

• *Eat 4 to 6 small meals a day. This enables your diaphragm to move freely and lets your lungs fill with air and empty out more easily*

• *If drinking liquids with meals makes you feel too full to eat, limit liquids with meals; drink an hour after meals.*

• *Consider adding a nutritional supplement at night time to avoid feeling full during the day*

Benefits of following COPD Nutritional Recommendations

COPD is a lung disease that causes a number of symptoms, including dyspnea (shortness of breath) and fatigue due to airway inflammation and narrowing.

There are a variety of benefits when it comes to following nutritional recommendations in COPD. Weight control, keeping your immune system healthy, helping your lungs heal from damage, maintaining your energy, and avoiding inflammation are among the ways your diet can enhance your health when you have this disease.

These effects won't reverse the condition, but they can help keep it from getting worse.

Weight Control

Weight is complicated when it comes to COPD. Obesity is considered a COPD risk factor. And being overweight places a high demand on your heart and lungs, making you short of breath and worsening your COPD symptoms.

But malnutrition and being underweight can pose a major problem in COPD too.2 Chronic disease puts increased demands on your body, robbing your body of nutrients. And, a lack of nutrients makes it even harder for you to heal from the recurrent lung damage inherent with COPD.

This means that weight control is something you need to be serious about. Regularly weighing yourself can help you get back on track quickly if you veer away from your ideal weight range. Strategic diet choices, of course, can help you stay on track.

Strengthening Your Immune System

Any infection, especially a respiratory one, can make it difficult to breathe and can lead to a COPD exacerbation.

When you have COPD, a pulmonary infection has a more severe impact on your already impaired lungs. And COPD itself results in a diminished ability to avoid infections through protective mechanisms like coughing.

Getting adequate nutrients like protein, vitamin C, and vitamin D through diet can help your immune system fight off infections.

Healing From Damage

Recurrent lung damage is the core problem in COPD. When your body is injured, it needs to heal. Nutrients like vitamin E and vitamin K help your body repair itself.

Maintaining Energy

COPD leads to low energy. You need to consume carbohydrates to fuel yourself.

Iodine, an essential mineral, helps your body make thyroid hormone to regulate your energy metabolism. Your body also needs adequate vitamin B12 and iron to keep your oxygen-carrying red blood cells healthy.

Avoiding Inflammation

Inflammation plays a major role in COPD. Experts recommend a diet rich in antioxidants such as plant-based foods and omega-3 fatty acid-rich seafood to help combat excessive inflammation.

Research also suggests that artificial preservatives may induce an inflammatory response that promotes diseases such as COPD, so they should be avoided.

How a COPD Diet Plan Works

A COPD diet plan is fairly flexible and can include many foods that you like to eat. General guidelines include:

• Avoiding allergy and asthma triggers

• Eliminating (or at least minimizing) processed foods

• Including fruits, vegetables, beans, nuts, dairy, lean meats, and seafood

You can follow a vegetarian or vegan diet if you want to, but you will need to make sure that you get enough fat and protein by eating things like avocados and healthy oils.

Duration

A COPD diet is meant to be followed for a lifetime. This is a chronic, incurable disease, and following these diet guidelines consistently can help you manage symptoms along the way.

What to Eat on a COPD Diet

There are plenty of options you can include in your diet when you have COPD. If you're having a hard time coming up a nutrition plan that is to your liking, a dietitian can help.

Fruit and Vegetables

Fresh or cooked fruits and vegetables are resources for essential vitamins and minerals. They also contain natural antioxidants that help promote healing and counteract inflammation. Consider the wide array of options, including potatoes, beets, spinach, carrots, broccoli, asparagus, bananas, peaches, blueberries, and grapes.

Energy-Rich Carbohydrates

You need a daily supply of energy, most of which comes from carbohydrate calories. Complex carbohydrates like whole grains can give you lasting energy. Simple carbohydrates like candy can give you a burst of energy, but then the excess calories are quickly stored as fat (leading to weight gain).

Consuming too much carbohydrate calories can lead to obesity and may increase your risk of diabetes. On the other hand, not consuming enough can leave you low in energy and underweight.

Make sure you get some professional guidance regarding your optimal calorie intake, which is calculated based on your age and height. Your COPD will also be considered, as it may mean that your body has a higher energy requirement.

According to the American Lung Association, your breathing muscles may need 10 times as many calories if you have COPD than breathing muscles of a person without the disease.

Proteins and Fats

Proteins are vital to your healing process, and they also help your body make immune cells. Foods like seafood, beef, poultry, pork, dairy, eggs, and beans contain protein.

Fats help you digest your food and make vitamins. Foods like meat, dairy, eggs, nuts, and oils contain fat.

Fiber

It's important to include enough fiber in your diet. While you might already know that fiber keeps your bowel movements regular and helps protect against colon cancer, a diet high in fiber is also associated with better lung function and reduced respiratory symptoms in people with COPD.

High-fiber foods include vegetables, legumes (beans and lentils), bran, whole grains, rice, cereals, whole-wheat pasta, and fresh fruit. These foods are also anti-inflammatory.

Your fiber consumption should be between approximately 21 and 38 grams of fiber each day, depending on your age and gender.

Beverages

Unless your doctor tells you otherwise, you should drink six to eight eight-ounce glasses of water daily. This helps to keep your mucus thin, making it easier to cough up.

It's easy to forget to drink, especially if you haven't been in the habit of hydrating. You might consider filling a large water bottle with your daily fluid requirements every morning and sipping on it throughout the day.

If plain water isn't palatable to you, and try warm or chilled herbal or green tea.

Alcohol can make you tired, especially if you are already chronically low in energy. And caffeine can raise your blood pressure or cause heart palpitations, making you feel light-headed, dizzy, or shorter of breath than usual. As some people with COPD may feel worse after consuming alcoholic or caffeinated beverages, it may be best to avoid or limit these.

Recommended Timing

Small, frequent calorie-dense meals can help you meet your caloric needs more efficiently if you are having a hard time keeping weight on. Small meals can also help you feel less full or bloated, making it more comfortable to breathe deeply.

Cooking Tips

You might enjoy keeping track of calories, reading nutrition labels, and coming up with new recipes. But not everyone wants to focus so much on every dietary detail or spend time working on creating a meal plan.

If you prefer to follow specific instructions for a personalized menu, talk to your doctor about getting a consultation with a nutritionist or a dietitian. You can get recipes or guidelines from a professional and ask questions about how to modify dishes to your preferences and for your disease.

Cooking guidelines to keep in mind include:

• Avoid deep-frying your food: This process creates trans fats, which can lead to additional cellular damage in your lungs beyond the damage that's already there due to COPD.

• Use salt in moderation: This is especially important if you have high blood pressure or edema (swelling of the feet or legs). Edema is a late-stage complication of COPD.

• Use fresh herbs to add natural flavor, which can reduce your reliance on salt.

• Use natural sweeteners like honey, ginger, or cinnamon instead of sugar. Excess sugar can increase the risk of edema.

Modifications

One of the most important dietary guidelines to keep in mind when you have COPD is avoiding foods that may trigger an allergic reaction or an asthma attack.

Allergies and asthma attacks can cause severe, sudden shortness of breath. Anything that triggers a bout of breathing problems can be life-threatening for you when you already have COPD.

Common food triggers include dairy products, eggs, nuts, or soybeans.

You don't need to avoid an allergen (a substance that causes an allergic reaction) if it doesn't cause you to have symptoms, but try to be observant about patterns and trends that exacerbate your symptoms.

If you notice that certain foods affect your breathing, it's important to be vigilant about avoiding them.

Considerations

The basics of a COPD diet are healthy guidelines for everyone. Because of your COPD, however, there are some additional things you should keep in mind when working to follow your eating plan.

Safety

Your tendency to cough when you have COPD could place you at risk of choking when you eat or drink. Be sure to give yourself ample time to consume your food and liquids carefully. Avoid talking while you are eating and drinking so you can reduce your risk of choking.

Shortness of breath can be a problem when eating too. Pace yourself and stick to foods that are not difficult for you to chew and swallow.

If you are on continuous oxygen therapy, make sure you use it while you eat. Since your body requires energy to eat and digest food, you will need to keep breathing in your supplemental oxygen to help you get through your meals.

SECTION 3: RECIPES

Breakfast Recipes

Ginger Apple Muffins
Ingredients:
- All-purpose flour (2 cups)
- Sugar or sugar-free sweeteners (2/3 cup)
- Baking powder (1 tbsp.)
- Salt (1/2 tsp.)
- Ground cinnamon (1 tsp.)
- Ground ginger (1 tsp.)
- Unsweetened almond milk (3/4 cup) - To make almond milk, you'll need to soak almonds in water for 1 – 2 days, drain and rinse them, then grind them with fresh water in a blender.
- Shredded apple (1 cup)
- Mashed ripe banana (1/2 cup)
- Apple cider vinegar (1 tbsp.)

Instructions::
1. Pre-heat the oven to 400'F.
2. Lightly grease the molds in a muffin pan, or use parchment paper to line up the molds.

3. Whisk together the flour, sugar, baking powder, salt, cinnamon and ginger in a mixing bowl until you form a smooth batter without any lumps.
4. In another mixing bowl, mix the almond milk, shredded apples, mashed banana and apple cider vinegar until the mixture is fully combined. Add the flour mixture and stir until the batter incorporates the milk mixture.
5. Fill the batter into the muffin molds, until the molds are 2/3 full.
6. Bake the muffins into the oven at 400'F for 15 – 20 minutes. When you insert a toothpick into a muffin and it comes clean, they are ready.
7. The ginger apple muffins yield 12 servings, with each muffin at approximately 170 calories. It has 0.6 mg fat, zero cholesterol, and 234 mg sodium.

Spinach and Mushroom Frittatas
Ingredients:
- Sliced button mushrooms (1 lb.)
- Chopped large onion (1 pc.)

- Chopped garlic (1 tbsp.)
- Spinach (1 lb.)
- Water (1/4 cup)
- Egg whites (6 pcs.)
- Eggs (4 pcs.)
- Firm tofu (6 oz.)
- Ground turmeric (1/2 tsp.)
- Kosher salt (1/2 tsp.)
- Cracked or powdered black pepper (1/2 tsp.)

Instructions:

1. Pre-heat the oven to 350'F.
2. In a non-stick skillet or sauté pan, sauté the button mushrooms over medium to high heat. Add chopped onions and keep sautéing for 3 minutes or until the onions are tender.
3. Add water. Then add spinach to the skillet or pan and cook for 2 minutes with the lid on, or until the spinach wilts. Cook again until all the water is dispersed. Set aside.
4. Puree, eggs, turmeric, salt, pepper, tofu and egg whites in a blender at medium or high speed until the mixture is smooth.

5. Gently pour the egg mixture into the spinach.
6. Bake the sauté pan into the oven for 25 – 30 minutes at 350'F. Once it's done, take the pan out, invert the frittata onto a plate and leave it for 10 minutes. Once it's done, cut the frittata into wedges and they're ready to be served.

Gluten-Free Strawberry Crepes
Ingredients:
- Sliced strawberries (6 cups)
- Sugar or honey (2 tbsp.)
- Large eggs (4 pcs.)
- Unsweetened almond milk (1 cup)
- Olive oil (2 tbsp.)
- Vanilla extract (1 tsp.)
- Light brown sugar (1 tsp.)
- Salt (1 tsp.)
- Gluten-free flour baking mix (3/4 cup)

Instructions:
1. Mix strawberries and sugar until the strawberries are coated. Let it stand for 30 minutes at room temperature.
2. Put the eggs, almond milk, olive oil, vanilla extract, brown sugar and salt

into a mixing bowl, then whisk it all together until all the ingredients are combined.

3. Add the gluten-free four and mix it until the batter is smooth and creamy.
4. Heat a non-stick skillet or crepe pan in a stove or oven on medium heat. Add ¼ cup of batter into the skillet and coat it evenly. Cook it for around 45 seconds or until the crepe starts to turn brown.
5. Flip the crepe over and cook the other side for 10 seconds then transfer it to a serving plate.
6. Take out ½ cup of the sugared strawberries with a spoon then put it on top of the crepe. Carefully fold the crepe as you cover the strawberries, in order to form a half-circle.
7. Drizzle the crepe with any syrup or juice then serve.

Cherry Quinoa Porridge
Ingredients:
- Water (1 cup)
- Dry quinoa (1/2 cup)
- Dried unsweetened cherries (1/2 cup)

- Vanilla extract (1/2 tsp.)
- Ground cinnamon (1/4 tsp.)
- Honey (1 tsp.)

Instructions:

1. Stir together water, quinoa, cherries, vanilla extract and cinnamon in a medium-sized saucepan. Bring it to a boil over medium or high heat.
2. Simmer with the lid covering the saucepan for 15 minutes. The quinoa is ready when all the water has been absorbed and the porridge is tender.
3. Drizzle with honey then serve.

Raspberry Green Tea Smoothie

Ingredients:

- Chilled green tea (1 ½ cups)
- Frozen unsweetened raspberries (2 cups)
- Banana (1 pc.)
- Honey (1 tbsp.) Protein powder (1/4 cup)

Instructions:

1. Add all the ingredients into a blender.
2. Puree the ingredients until the mixture is very smooth and creamy.

3. Pour the puree into a tall glass and serve.

Buckwheat and Quinoa Granola

Ingredients:
- Honey (3 tbsp.)
- Liquid coconut oil (3 tbsp.)
- Vanilla extract (1 tsp.)
- Ground cinnamon (1/4 tsp.)
- Ground ginger (1/4 tsp.)
- Buckwheat oats (1 cup)
- Cooked quinoa (1 cup)
- Regular oats (1/2 cup)
- Dried unsweetened cranberries (1/2 cup)

Instructions:
1. Line a baking sheet with parchment paper or silicon baking mat, or lightly grease a sheet with olive oil. Preheat the oven to 325'F.
2. Stir together coconut oil, vanilla extract, honey, ginger and cinnamon into a small mixing bowl.
3. In a separate large mixing bowl, mix the buckwheat, quinoa and oats together.

4. Add the honey mixture and stir thoroughly until all the ingredients are fully combined.
5. Spread the mixture evenly in a pan and bake at 325'F for 40 – 45 minutes or until it begins to brown.
6. Remove the pan and add the cranberries. Stir it well then place the pan on a cooling rack for it to cool completely.
7. Store the granola in an airtight container.

Cherry Quinoa Porridge
Ingredients:
- Water (1 cup)
- Dry quinoa (1 cup)
- Dried unsweetened cherries (1 cup)
- Vanilla extract (1/2 tsp)
- Ground cinnamon (¼ tsp)
- Honey (¼ tsp), optional

Instructions:
1. Get a medium-sized saucepan and stir all the ingredients (except honey) together. Over medium-high heat, bring everything to a boil.

2. Lower the heat, cover the saucepan and simmer. Wait for 15 minutes or until the water is completely absorbed and the quinoa is all tender.
3. If desired, drizzle with some honey before serving.

Gingerbread Oatmeal

Ingredients:
• Water (1 cup)
• Old-fashioned oats (½ cup)
• Dried, unsweetened cranberries or cherries (¼ cup)
• Ground ginger (1 tsp)
• Ground cinnamon (½ teaspoon)
• Ground nutmeg (¼ teaspoon)
• Flaxseeds (1 tablespoon) Molasses (1 tablespoon)

Instructions:
1. Mix the water, oats, cranberries or cherries, ginger, cinnamon, and nutmeg in a small-sized saucepan and heat over medium high settings. Bring the mixture into a boil, then reduce the heat. Simmer for 5 minutes or until such time

that the water has been almost completely absorbed.
2. Put the flaxseeds, then cover the saucepan. Let the mixture stand for another 5 minutes.
3. Drizzle the dish with some molasses before serving.

Spanish Frittata
Ingredients (for the frittata):
- Large organic eggs (1 dozen)
- Coconut milk (½ cup)
- Sea salt (½ tsp, or more to taste)
- Extra-virgin olive oil or coconut oil (2 tbsp)
- Small, finely chopped red onion (1 pc)
- Sautéed mushrooms or vegetable of your choice (½ cup) Spinach or arugula (1 cup)

Instructions:
1. Pre-heat the oven set at a temperature of 375ºF.
2. Whisk the coconut milk and eggs together as you sprinkle two pinches of salt; then set aside.

3. Get a pan and heat coconut oil at medium-high setting. Sauté onions for about 3 minutes or until translucent. Add the mushrooms or vegetables of your choice and sauté until they soften. Put the spinach in and fold into the vegetable mixture just until they wilt. Remove the veggies from the pan and set aside.

4. Adjust the heat to low setting, while adding just a bit more coconut oil, if necessary. With the same skillet, place the eggs while shaking to evenly distribute the mixture. Set the heat to medium-low then cook for about 5 more minutes. Use a spatula to gather the eggs at the edges and mix them with the rest of the ingredients at the center. Do this until there are no more runny edges. Arrange the veggie mix evenly over the top.

5. Move the dish to the oven and resume cooking for 5 more minutes or until it is set and browned slightly. Turn off the heat and take the dish out of the oven; be wary of the hot handle as you do this

so it is best to wear oven mitts first. Finish everything off by sliding the slightly cooked frittata onto a big serving plate. Place a plate on top of the pan. Hold together the pan and the plate then invert them in a way that the frittata falls on the plate. Slide it back to the pan so that the slightly cooked side is on top. Put the dish back into the oven and cook for another 3 or 4 minutes. Serve with a simple siding of salad with citrus vinaigrette.

Orange Apple Breakfast Shake
Ingredients
- Almonds (2 tbsp.)
- Apple slices (1/2 cup)
- Orange sections (1/2 cup)
- 2% milk (1 cup)
- Zone Protein Powder (14g)

Instructions:
1. Place all ingredients together in the blender. Mix until everything is wellincorporated and smooth.

2. Pour the contents of the blender into a tall glass.
3. Serve and enjoy!

Chocolate Cherry Shake

Ingredients:

- Unprocessed, unsweetened cocoa powder (1 tbsp.)
- Frozen dark cherries, pitted (½ cup)
- Coconut, almond or flax milk (1 cup)
- Pure vanilla extract; a few drops of liquid stevia preferably Sweet Leaf Vanilla
- Crème (½ tsp) Ice cubes, if desired

Instructions:

1. Mix all the ingredients in a blender. Process until everything is smooth.
2. Pour in a tall glass.
3. Serve and enjoy!

Oatmeal Spiced with Apple Pie

Ingredients:

- Water (3 cups)
- Steel Cut Oats (3/4 cup)
- Pumpkin Spice - Pumpkin Pie Spice (2 tsp)

- Zone Protein Powder (70 grams)
- Applesauce (1 cup)
- Stevia Extract (1 tsp, to taste)
- 16 Pecans or walnuts (16 pcs – halves)

Instructions:

1. Boil the water before stirring in the pumpkin pie spice and steel-cut oats.
1. Cook for about 5 minutes then reduce the heat. Simmer for half an hour. Let the dish col off before stirring in the protein powder. (This can be prepared the previous evening, refrigerate, and then just heat in the microwave oven the following morning.) Add the rest of the ingredients once you are about to eat.
2. If prepared the previous night, take the dish out of the refrigerator and pour into 4 individual bowls. Distribute the rest of the ingredients among the 4 bowls and warm up in the microwave oven for 2 ½ minutes under high temperature setting. Stir while halfway through.

Eggs and Apple Pork withStrawberries

Ingredients:

- Olive oil (1 1/2 tsps - divided)
- Boneless center-cut loin pork chops (2 oz)
- Salt & pepper, to taste
- Small apple, sliced (1 pc)
- Cinnamon (1/4 tsp)
- Egg whites (1/2 cup) Strawberries, sliced (1 cup)

Instructions:

1. Heat half a teaspoon of olive oil in a large skillet under medium-high. Place the salt & pepper-seasoned pork, and the cinnamon-seasoned apple slices on opposite sides of the skillet. Cook until the pork is no longer pinkish and the apple slices are just a bit soft.
2. Remove the pork and apple slices from the skillet, and set aside. Keep warm.
3. Heat the remaining 1 tsp of olive oil and scramble the egg whites.
4. Garnish the dish with some sliced strawberries on the side.
5. Serve and enjoy!

Eggs and Fruit Salad
Ingredients:

- Strawberries, sliced (1/2 cup)
- Mandarin orange sections, unsweetened or fresh (1/2 cup)
- Blueberries (1/2 cup)
- Egg whites (6 hardboiled eggs, discard yolks)
- Avocado (1/2 cup) Salsa (3 tbsp.)

Instructions:

1. Prepare the fruit salad in a medium-sized bowl. Slice strawberries, and then gently stir blueberries and mandarin sections in.
2. Boil the eggs for about 10 minutes, then allow to cool. Halve the eggs and remove the yolks.
3. Dice the hardboiled egg whites and avocado; mix in a separate bowl. Stir the salsa in.
4. Put some fruit salad sidings, and serve.

Ham & Onion Frittata withFruit Salad

Ingredients:

- Cooking spray (olive oil)
- Onion, chopped (1 pc)
- Canadian bacon, cut in bite sized pieces (4 oz)

- Egg whites (2 cups)
- Olive oil (1 tbsp.)
- 1% milk (1/4 cup)
- Dried dill (1 tbsp or 3 tbsp if fresh)
- Salt and pepper, to taste
- Mozzarella cheese, shredded (3/4 cup)
- Parmesan cheese, grated (1/4 cup)
- Blueberries (1 cup, divided)
- Freshly squeezed lemon juice (3 tbsp)
- Vanilla 1 1/2 tsps
- Agave nectar (1 ½ tbsp.)
- Peach, sliced (1 pc)
- Pear, sliced (1pc)
- Strawberries, sliced (1 ½ cups)

Instructions:

1. Spray olive oil in a large ovenproof skillet. Saute the ham and onion until the onion is cooked and golden. Set them aside.
2. Pre-heat the oven for broiling.
3. Whisk together the egg whites, milk, olive oil, dill, and salt & pepper in a medium-sized bowl. Add the cheeses into the mix.
4. Spread the cooled ham and onion evenly at the bottom of the skillet. Top

with the egg mixture. Cook under medium heat setting until the bottom settles.

5. Put the skillet under broiler, and then cook some more until the eggs are set and the top is golden brown. Remove the skillet from the oven and set it aside and allow to cool off.

6. Take ¼ cup of blueberries and mix with vanilla, agave nectar, and lemon juice in a small-sized bowl. Set the mixture aside.

7. Mix the sliced fruits and blueberries in a large-sized bowl. Pour the sauce mixture over the fruits and mix everything up.

8. Serve and enjoy with the frittata.

Grapefruit Breakfast

Ingredients:
- Canadian bacon (2 slices)
- Grapefruit (1 pc)
- 0%-fat Greek yogurt (1/2 cup)
- Blueberries (1/3 cup) Sliced almonds (3 1/2 tbsp.)

Instructions:

1. Get the slices of Canadian bacon and cut into smaller pieces. Place in the microwave oven to warm.
2. Cut the grapefruit into two, then slice each section into smaller pieces. Place the pieces in a bowl. Stir the Canadian bacon in.
3. Next, get another bowl and mix the almonds and blueberries with yogurt.
4. Combine the contents of the two bowls and mix well. Serve and enjoy!

Five-Minute Breakfast
Ingredients
- 1 cup leftover cooked brown rice
- ¼ cup sunflower seeds
- ¼ teaspoon cinnamon powder
- ½ cup rice milk or other alternative milk
- 1/8 cup raisins
- ¼ teaspoon carob powder (optional)
- ¼ cup chopped walnuts
- ½ teaspoon maple syrup (optional)

Instructions:
1. Combine all ingredients in a saucepan on the stove.

2. Add milk to cover the rice for a cereal consistency.
3. Warm over moderate heat to desired temperature and serve.

Broccoli and Olive Frittata

This is a great-tasting, crustless alternative to quiche.

- Ingredients
- 1 medium yellow bell pepper
- 1 medium red bell pepper
- 2 broccoli crowns, cut into bite-size pieces
- ½ cup pitted ripe olives, halved
- 6 organic eggs, softly beaten
- ½ cup soy milk
- 2 tablespoons chopped fresh sweet basil or 1 teaspoon dried basil
- 1 teaspoon dried oregano
- Sea salt and pepper to taste
- ¼ cup cashews, ground fine for garnish

Instructions:

1. Quarter and seed peppers, then broil them for 5–10 minutes or until lightly charred.

2. Place in a closed brown paper bag, and let cool for 5 minutes. Peel and thinly slice. (If you don't mind the peel, leave it on and just slice the roasted peppers into thin slices.) Reduce oven heat to 400° F.
3. Grease a 9-inch round pan. Place broccoli, peppers, and olives in the pan, making sure to arrange them evenly. Beat remaining ingredients together in a small bowl and pour over vegetables.
4. Bake for 35–40 minutes or until the center has set. Broil for the last two minutes to brown the top. Cool, slice into wedges, and serve warm or cold garnished with ground cashews (in place of Parmesan cheese).

Granola

Ingredients
- cups rolled oats
- 1¼ cups unsweetened coconut
- 1 cup chopped almonds
- 1 cup raw, shelled sunflower seeds
- ½ cup sesame seeds
- ½ cup honey

- ½ cup organic coconut oil

Instructions:

1. Preheat oven to 325° F.
2. Mix dry ingredients together in a large bowl.
3. Combine honey and oil in a saucepan and heat to a liquid consistency.
4. Pour over dry ingredients. Mix well. Flatten into a baking pan.
5. Bake for 15–20 minutes. Cool and store

Mexican Morning Eggs

Ingredients

- organic eggs, cooked any way you like
- 1 cup leftover cooked brown rice
- ¾ cup black beans, home-cooked or from a can (rinse first to remove excess salt)
- ½ teaspoon cumin
- ½ teaspoon paprika
- ½ teaspoon chili powder
- ½ teaspoon sea salt
- 1 medium avocado, diced

Instructions:

1. Combine rice, beans, and seasonings in a skillet; cook over medium-low heat.

2. In a separate skillet, prepare eggs however you desire.
3. When eggs are finished and rice and beans are warm, serve them together on a plate. Add diced avocado on top.

Protein Power Breakfast
Ingredients
- 1 tablespoon flaxseeds
- 2 tablespoons sesame seeds
- 2 tablespoons sunflower seeds
- 1 teaspoon honey
- ½ medium banana, sliced

Instructions:
1. Grind all seeds together in your coffee grinder (which by now must be going through an identity crisis).
2. Place seeds in a cereal bowl. Add honey and a small amount of hot water or hot milk substitute. Mix together and top with sliced bananas.
3. Sprinkle a little more honey or maple syrup on top and enjoy.

Quickest Oatmeal You'll Ever Eat

Ingredients

- 1 cup nut-and-fruit muesli (natural with no additives)
- ½–1 cup hot or boiling water
- ½ teaspoon maple syrup (optional; the fruit in the cereal adds sweetness)

Instructions:

1. Stir all ingredients together in a cereal bowl.
2. Let sit for at least 1 minute before eating.

Tofu Scramble

Ingredients

- 1 pound firm tofu
- tablespoons spelt flour (orany type of nonwheat flour)
- 1 tablespoon olive oil, for sautéing
- 4–5 cups chopped mixed vegetables (for example, zucchini, yellow squash, carrots, onions, and garlic)
- 1 teaspoon onion powder
- 1 teaspoon paprika
- 2 teaspoons garlic powder
- ½ teaspoon sea salt

- ½ teaspoon turmeric
- 1 teaspoon curry powder
- Black pepper to taste
- Dash cayenne if tolerated
- ½ cup filtered water

Instructions:

1. Drain tofu of extra moisture and cut into slabs.
2. Mix spices and flour together in a small bowl.
3. If using garlic and onions, sauté them together in a large skillet over medium heat until they are soft. Add other vegetables, and continue sautéing until they are partially cooked.
4. Add tofu by crumbling it into pieces to resemble scrambled eggs.
5. Add spice/flour mixture and water.
6. Sauté a little longer until vegetables are cooked to your liking. (Make sure to cook flour long enough to eliminate the taste of raw starch—about 2 minutes). Serve immediately.

Wheat-Free Pancakes

Ingredients

- ½ cup walnuts, ground in food processor to a fine powder
- ¾ cup spelt flour
- ¾ cup rice flour
- 1 teaspoon cream of tartar
- 1 teaspoon baking soda
- ¾ teaspoon sea salt
- 11/3 cup water
- 1 tablespoon olive oil

Optional—sprinkle fresh berries, chopped apple, Instructions:

1. Combine ground walnuts, flours, salt, cream of tartar, baking soda, and salt in a medium-sized mixing bowl, blending well.
2. Whisk 1 cup of water into dry ingredients, then gradually add the rest of the water to reach desired consistency. Add more water if the batter is still too thick. Stir in any optional ingredients until just combined.
3. Brush or spray a large skillet or griddle with small amount of oil. Heat skillet or griddle over medium heat. Drop batter

onto hot cooking surface using a large spoon. Cook the pancake until bubbles form on top; flip. Cook on the second side until lightly browned.

Easy Pancakes

Ingredients
- tablespoons raw sunflower seeds, ground fine 3 tablespoons raw pumpkin seeds, ground fine
- organic eggs
- ¼ cup nongluten oat flour (any nonwheat or nongluten flour will do)
- ¼ cup rice milk
- ¼ cup blueberries (optional)

Instructions:
1. Combine all ingredients in a medium-sized bowl and mix well until clumps have dissolved.
2. Heat a lightly oiled skillet or griddle pan over medium heat.
3. Pour batter into 3-inch diameter circles in the pan. When pancakes begin to bubble, flip and cook on the other side for a short amount of time until lightly browned on both sides.

Breakfast Eggnog

Ingredients
- organic eggs
- 1 cup rice milk, chilled
- 1 tablespoon vanilla extract
- Dash cinnamon
- Dash nutmeg

Instructions:
1. Combine all ingredients in a large cup or bowl, and mix well until mixture looks uniform.
2. Strain mixture through small strainer into a serving glass and serve.

Breakfast Smoothie

Ingredients
- tablespoons soy protein powder
- 1 cup organic frozen berries (blueberries, strawberries, raspberries,blackberries, cherries)
- 1 cups soy milk (use water if you prefer, or half water and half milk)

Instructions:
1. Place all ingredients in blender and blend to desired thickness and consistency.

Roasted Chicken Wraps

Ingredients:

- Low-fat or reduced-fat mayonnaise (1/2 cup)
- Pickle juice (2 tbsp.)
- Freshly cracked black pepper (1 tsp.)
- Shredded red cabbage (1 ½ cups)
- Apple cider vinegar (1 tbsp.)
- Kosher salt (1/4 tsp.)
- Cayenne pepper (1/4 tsp.)
- Cooled deli roasted chicken (1 whole)
- Wheat, whole-wheat or mixed-grain flatbreads (6 pcs.)

Instructions:

1. Mix pickle juice, pepper and mayonnaise in a mixing bowl. Put the mixture into the refrigerator to set aside.
2. Meanwhile, add salt, vinegar, cabbage and cayenne pepper into a separate mixing bowl. Toss the cabbage to mix it with the other ingredients.
3. Discard skin and bones from the roasted chicken and shred the chicken into bite-sized pieces.

4. Add the chicken into the mayonnaise mixture and combine it.
5. Arrange the cabbage and the chicken evenly in the flatbread slices and roll it tightly.
6. You can either eat it on its own, or heat it using a toaster oven or microwave oven.

Lentil and Garbanzo Soup

Ingredients:
- Chopped onions (2 pcs.)
- Chopped celery (1 cup)
- Diced carrots (1 cup)
- Grated ginger (2 tsp.)
- Minced garlic (1 tsp.)
- Garam masala (1 tsp.)
- Turmeric (1 tsp.)
- Ground cumin (1/2 tsp.)
- Ground cayenne pepper (1/4 tsp.)
- Vegetable broth or stock (6 cups)
- Lentils (1 cup)
- Rinsed and drained garbanzo beans (2 15-oz. cans) Undrained petite diced tomatoes (1 14.5-oz. can)

Instructions:

1. Sauté onions in a large pot over medium to high heat for 3 – 4 minutes or until onions are tender.
2. Add celery and carrots into the pot and keep cooking for an additional five minutes. Stir in garlic, garam masala, turmeric, cumin and cayenne pepper into the pot and keep cooking for 30 more seconds.
3. Add the cups of broth, lentils, garbanzo beans and tomatoes into the pot, then keep stirring the ingredients until all of them are combined. Cook the broth for 90 minutes or until the lentils are tender.
4. For a creamier and thicker soup, you can take out half of the broth, puree it with a food processor, then put it back into the pot and stir.

Roasted Sweet Potato Soup
Ingredients:
- Sweet potatoes (2 ½ lbs.)
- Extra-virgin olive oil (1 tbsp.)
- Kosher salt (1/4 tsp.)

- Freshly cracked pepper (1/2 tsp.)
- Sliced leek or onions (1 ½ cups)
- Minced garlic (1 tsp.)
- White wine (1/2 cup)
- Chopped thyme leaves (1 tsp.)
- Vegetable broth (5 cups) Orange juice (2 cups)

Instructions:

1. Pre-heat the oven to 400'F. Peel and cut sweet potatoes into very small pieces.
2. Place the sweet potatoes on a baking sheet and toss them with pepper, olive oil and salt. Roast the potatoes in the oven for 45 – 50 minutes at 400'F or until the sweet potatoes are well browned. Set aside.
3. In a large soup pot, cook the leeks or onions over medium to high heat for 8 minutes or until they are tender. Add ginger and garlic, stir and cook for one more minute. Add the white wine and bring it to a boil until the wine evaporates.
4. When all the wine has evaporated, add the vegetable broth, thyme and sweet potatoes then bring the whole soup

mixture into a boil. Turn down the heat and let it simmer for 20 minutes or until the vegetables are soft and tender.

5. Use a blender to puree the soup in batches. Reheat each batch of soup before serving.

Kipper (Smoked Herring) Salad

Ingredients:

- Low-fat or reduced-fat mayonnaise (1/2 cup)
- Finely chopped small onion (1 pc.)
- Finely chopped celery stalk (1 pc.)
- Chopped parsley (1 tbsp.)
- Lemon juice (1 tsp.)
- Minced garlic (1 clove)
- Salt (1/8 tsp.)
- Ground black pepper (1/8 tsp.)
- Drained kippers or smoked herring (1 6-oz. pc.)

Instructions:

1. Stir together all the ingredients except kipper in a medium-sized bowl.
2. Add flaked kippers into the mixture and gently toss them.

3. Refrigerate once the salad is done. You can use it as a sandwich filling or as a side dish to your main course.

Quick-and-Easy Pumpkin Soup

Ingredients:

- Chopped onion (1 cup)
- Peeled and minced gingerroot (1 1-inch pc.)
- Minced garlic (1 clove)
- Vegetable stock (6 cups)
- Pumpkin puree (4 cups)
- Salt (1 tsp.)
- Chopped thyme (1/2 tsp.)
- Half-and-half milk (1/2 cup)
- Chopped parsley (1 tsp.)

Instructions:

1. Put garlic, ginger and onion in a large soup pot. Add ½ cup of vegetable stock and cook for 5 minutes or until onion is tender.
2. Add thyme, salt, 5 ½ cups of vegetable stock and pumpkin puree into the pot. Cook the soup for 30 minutes.
3. Puree the soup using a handheld blender until it becomes smooth.

4. Take out the soup from the stove and add half-and-half milk. Stir it well, then add chopped parsley as garnish. Serve.

Persimmon and Pear Salad
Ingredients:
- Whole-grain mustard (1 tsp.)
- Lemon juice (2 tbsp.)
- Extra virgin olive oil (3 tbsp.)
- Minced shallot (1 pc.)
- Minced garlic (1 tsp.)
- Sliced ripe persimmon (1 pc.)
- Sliced ripe pear (1 pc.)
- Toasted and chopped pecans (1/2 cup) Baby spinach (6 cups)

Instructions:
1. Whisk together shallot, garlic, mustard, lemon juice and olive oil in a salad bowl.
2. Add persimmon, spinach, pecans and pear into the salad mixture. Toss well to coat the fruits and vegetables.
3. Serve immediately. Store the remainder in an airtight container.

Smoked Trout Tartine

Ingredients:

- Freshly squeezed lemon juice (2 tbsp)
- Extra-virgin olive oil (1 tsp)
- Dijon mustard (1 tsp)
- Sugar (1 pinch)
- Smoked trout, flaked into small bite-size pieces (¾ pound)
- Capers, rinsed and drained (2 tsp)
- Diced roasted red peppers (½ cup)
- Cannellini (white kidney), drained and rinsed (½ can - 15-ounce)
- Celery, finely chopped (1 stalk)
- Minced onion (2 tsp)
- Chopped fresh dill (1 tsp), or dried dill ((½ tsp.)
- Crusty, toasted whole-grain bread (4 large, half-inch slices)
- Garnish: dill sprigs

Instructions:

1. Get a large bowl and whisk the lemon juice, olive oil, mustard, and sugar together. Then add in the rest of the ingredients, except for the bread. Toss everything to mix properly.

2. Take a slice of bread and place it on a serving plate. Spoon some trout mixture on top. If desired, garnish it with dill sprigs.

Tropical Quinoa Salad withCashew Nuts
Ingredients (for the quinoa):
- Dried quinoa, rinsed well (1 cup)
- Red onion, finely chopped (½ pc)
- Apple or carrot, finely chopped (1 cup)
- Lime juice (from 1 lime)
- Honey or agave (2 tbsp.)
- Extra-virgin olive oil (1 tbsp.)
- Large mango, chopped (1 pc; not overly ripe)
- Mint, finely chopped (¼ cup)
- Sea salt, just to taste (1 tsp)
- Freshly ground black pepper, just to taste
- Ginger, finely chopped (½" pc)
- Avocado, chopped or thinly sliced (1 pc)
- Cashew nuts, coarsely chopped (1 cup)
- Romaine lettuce or preferred greens, roughly chopped (3 cups)

Instructions:

1. To cook the quinoa, put 2 cups of water in a medium-sized saucepan and bring to a boil. Add the quinoa. Cover the saucepan and simmer for around 15 to 20 minutes. Set the dish aside and let it cool, spreading it out to achieve best results.
2. Get a large bowl and toss in the chopped apple or carrot, and red onion. Whisk the lime juice, olive oil, and honey together before tossing into the bowl. Next, add the cooked and cooled quinoa to the bowl, followed by the mango. Toss well.
3. Add the cilantro, ginger, mint, and salt and pepper (to taste) into the mix. Garnish with chopped cashews and sliced avocado.
4. Scoop the mixture over greens. Serve at room temperature or chilled.

Applesauce Burger withSpinach Salad

Ingredients:

- Unsweetened applesauce, or chunk style if unavailable (1/3 cup)

- Old fashioned oats (3 tbsp)
- Dehydrated onion flakes (2 tsp, to taste)
- Chili powder (1/2 tsp)
- Ground chicken breast (3 oz)
- Dressing & Spinach Salad
- Olive oil (1 1/2 tsps0
- Vinegar (2 tsp)
- Water (2 tsp)
- Sugar free All Fruit - or any preferred flavor (1 tsp)
- Salt & pepper, to taste
- Baby spinach, stems torn off (3 cups)
- Red onion - roughly chopped (2 slices)
- Tomato, cut (1/2 pc)
- Strawberries, cut into chunks or just crush a few pieces to enhance the dressing (1/2 cup)

Instructions:

1. Pre-heat the broiler.
2. Mix together the egg whites, oatmeal, onions. and ¼ cup applesauce. Add the chicken. Mix everything well and make a burger patty.
3. Spray non-stick coating on broiler pan. Place the burger on the rack and broil

for about 5 minutes before turning over. Broil for another 5 minutes or until the meat is no longer pinkish in color.

4. Heat the rest of the applesauce and pour over the burger. (Experiment with the amounts of applesauce and oatmeal until your reach the desired consistency.)

5. While the burger is still cooking, whisk together some dressing ingredients with some mashed strawberries.

6. Get a salad bowl and mix the tomato, onion, and strawberries together. Drizzle with dressing. Serve.

Quick Chicken Stir-Fry

Ingredients:
- Olive oil (1 1/2 tsp)
- Broccoli florets (2 cups)
- Chopped onion (3/4 cup)
- Snow peas (3/4 cup)
- Garlic, pressed (1 clove)
- Boneless chicken breast, cut to bite-size pieces (3 oz.)
- Garbanzo beans, low sodium, rinsed and drained (1/4 cup) Salsa (1/4 cup)

Instructions:

1. Pre-heat the wok under medium temperature, then heat 1 tsp of olive oil.
2. Mix the vegetables and stir fry for about 2 minutes or until defrosted and hot. Remove the veggies, put in a bowl, and set aside. Heat the rest of the oil in the wok.
3. In the hot oil, press a clove of garlic, then put the chicken in, stir fry for around 4 minutes or until done.
4. Put back the cooked veggies together with the garbanzo beans into the wok. Toss everything together for 2 more minutes. Serve with some salsa on the side.

Asparagus Frittata with Fruit

Ingredients:

- Olive oil, divided (2 tbsp.)
- Onion, minced (1 1/2 cups)
- Asparagus, snapped off tough ends, spears diagonally cut into 1" lengths (2 lbs)
- Egg, lightly beaten (1 pc)
- Egg whites (2 cups)

- Salt & pepper, to taste
- Low-fat Swiss cheese, grated (4 oz.)
- Mandarin orange sections (1 cup, in water) Blueberries (2 cups)

Instructions:

1. Heat 1 ½ tbsp. of olive oil under medium high heat in a 10" ovenproof frying pan.
2. Put the onions in and cook until soft for about 3 minutes.
3. Toss in the asparagus; reduce heat setting to medium low. Cover and cook for another 3 minutes.
4. Beat the egg whites after adding salt & pepper, and ½ tbsp. of oil. Pour the mix into the pan and allow to cook until the bottom is almost set, but the top is still runny. Pre-heat the oven broiler while cooking.
5. Sprinkle some cheese over the eggs and broil for about 4 to 6 minutes or until the cheese is brown and melted.
6. While cooking the frittata, divide the fruits evenly into 4 bowls. Take the frittata out of the oven and slide into a

serving dish.   Cut into wedges, then serve.

Arlecchino Salad
Ingredients:
- Extra virgin olive oil (1 1/2 tsp.)
- Freshly squeezed lemon juice (3 tbsp.)
- Lemon pepper (1 tsp)
- Romaine lettuce, ripped (2 cups)
- Strawberries, sliced (1 cup)
- Cucumber, sliced (1 1/2 cups, 150g)
- Cherry tomatoes, halved (1 cup)
- Mushrooms, sliced (1/2 cup)
- Cashew nuts, smashed (1 tsp)
- Chunk light tuna in water (3 oz.)
- Melba toast , crushed as croutons (2 pcs)

Instructions:
1. Whisk together the extra virgin oil, lemon pepper and lemon juice in a small-sized bowl to make the dressing.
2. Create a salad with the rest of the ingredients (including the toasts). Mix everything in a bowl, then top with the crushed melba toast.
3. Add the dressing before serving.

Baked Eggs withWilted Baby Spinach

Ingredients:

- Fresh squeezed lime juice (1 tbsp, to taste)
- Pear, cored (1 pc, halved)
- 0%-Fat Greek yogurt (1/2 cup)
- Vanilla extract (1 tsp)
- Blueberries (1/2 cup)
- Cooking spray
- Olive oil , divided (3 tsps)
- Diced shallots (1/4 cup)
- Baby spinach, withlarge stems removed (1 1/2 lbs)
- Egg whites (1 cup)
- Salt & pepper, to taste
- Parmesan or Asagio cheese, shredded (2 tbsp.)

Instructions:

1. Prepare the fruit salad first. Squeeze the lime juice into a regular-sized bowl, then add the cut pear. Stir in a way that the lime juice coats the pear. Mix vanilla with yogurt, using as much as necessary. Coat the pear with lime juice

again before adding to the yogurt. Put it aside and refrigerate.

2. Pre-heat the oven to a temperature of 4000F. Lightly spray 4 ramekins or oven-safe dishes with cooking spray. Over medium low setting, heat a large-sized skillet. Add shallots and 2 tsp of olive oil. Cook for around 2 to 3 minutes.

3. Add the spinach and salt & pepper. Cook until the spinach is wilted or around 2 to 3 minutes.

4. Put the cheese in, and then remove from heat. Evenly distribute the wilted spinach among the 4 oven-safe dishes, creating a well at the center of each dish.

5. Add 1 tsp of olive oil and a dash of salt & pepper with the egg whites. Divide evenly among the dishes.

6. Put the oven-safe dishes on 1 or 2 rimmed baking sheets. Bake for around 15 to 17 minutes or until set, or as desired.

7. Immediately serve with the fruit salad.

Balsamic Chicken, Tomatoes & White Bean Salad

Ingredients:

- Boneless skinless chicken breast (6 oz.)
- Salt & pepper, to taste
- Garlic, crushed (2 cloves)
- Whole grain mustard (1 tbsp.)
- Balsamic vinegar (2 tbsp.)
- Cooking spray, olive oil
- Cannellini beans, rinsed and drained (1/2 cup)
- Cherry tomatoes, halved (1 pint)
- Low-fat feta, crumbled (1/4 cup)
- Arugula leaves (6 cups)
- Lemon, cut into wedges, for serving (1 pc)
- Extra virgin olive oil (2 tsp)
- Applesauce (1 cup) Pumpkin pie spice (2 tsp)

Instructions:

1. Season the chicken with salt & pepper. Whisk some mustard, vinegar, and garlic in a ceramic dish. Coat the chicken with the mixture. Cover and place in refrigerator for 20 minutes or more.

2. Remove the chicken from the marinade. Warm skillet under high heat. Spray chicken lightly with oil. Cook until golden or around 1 minute for each side. Lower the heat to medium low setting.
3. Cook the chicken for around 6 to 8 minutes on both sides, or until the chicken is cooked through.
4. Set aside a mixture of olive oil and lemon seasoned with salt & pepper.
5. Move the chicken to a large plate. cover and allow to sit for around 5 minutes. Mix feta, tomato, beans, dressing, and arugula in a large-sized bowl. Toss everything gently, then divide into 2 plates.
6. Slice the chicken and garnish with salad. Scoop into plates, and season with pepper.
7. Top with applesauce and. Serve with dessert of pumpkin pie spice.

Chicken Barbecue Salad
Ingredients:
- Olive oil (2 tsp)

- Boneless chicken breast, diced (3 oz.)
- Bell peppers, strips (1 1/2 cups)
- Onions, diced (1/4 cup)
- Cider vinegar (1/8 tsp)
- Worcestershire sauce (1/8 tsp)
- Minced garlic (1 tsp)
- Zoned Barbecue Sauce (1/2 cup)
- Lettuce (3 cups)
- Shredded cabbage - (2 cups)
- Salt & pepper, to taste

Instructions:

1. Put the chicken breast, oil, pepper, vinegar, onion, garlic and
1. Worcestershire sauce in a saute pan. Cook until the chicken is brown and the veggies are tender, then add some Zoned barbecue sauce.
2. Cover the pan and allow to simmer for about 5 minutes or until hot, occasionally stirring to make sure the flavors blend well.
3. Mix shredded cabbage and lettuce together, and then put the saladcabbage mixture on a large-sized oval plate. Scoop the veggie mixture and chicken to the middle of the plate,

with the salad cabbage mixture underneath.

4. Sprinkle with a dash of salt & pepper, and then serve quickly.

Dinner Recipes

Steamed Salmon with Lemon-Scented Zucchini

Ingredients:

- Sliced onion (1 pc.)
- Sliced lemon (1 pc.)
- Sliced zucchini (2 pcs.)
- White wine (1 cup)
- Water (2 cups)
- Salmon fillets (4 6-ounce pcs.)
- Kosher salt (1/4 tsp.)
- Freshly ground pepper (1/4 tsp.)

Instructions:

1. In a large Dutch oven, place the lemon, zucchini, onion, water and wine at the bottom of the oven.
2. Season the salmon fillets with salt and pepper.
3. In the meantime, fit a steamer rack over the vegetables in the oven and place it in medium to high heat until the liquid starts to boil.
4. Reduce the heat from medium to low heat and carefully place the fillets in the rack. Cover the fillets and steam them

for 8 – 10 minutes or until they are cooked through.

5. Serve the fillets on top of the vegetables. Add poaching liquid and top it with sliced olives and garnish, if desired.

Sweet Potato and Black Bean Burgers with Lime Mayonnaise

Ingredients:

- Low-fat or reduced-fat mayonnaise (1/2 cup)
- Lime (1 pc.)
- Hot sauce (1/2 tsp.)
- Chopped small onion (1 pc.)
- Minced jalapeno (1 pc.)
- Ground cumin (2 tsp.)
- Minced garlic (2 tsp.)
- Drained and mashed black beans (214.5 oz. cans)
- Raw sweet potato (2 cups)
- Lightly beaten egg (1 pc.)
- Plain breadcrumbs (1 cup) Whole-wheat hamburger buns

Instructions:
1. Set the oven rack 4 – 5 inches from the broiler then preheat the broiler at medium to high heat.
2. Squeeze one lime into a mixing bowl and hot sauce and mayonnaise into the bowl. Stir the three ingredients well then refrigerate the mixture to set aside.
3. Heat a large skillet in medium to high heat. Add the onion and cook for 3 – 4 minutes or until the onion is tender. Add the garlic, jalapeno and cumin then cook for 30 seconds.
4. Add sweet potato, mashed beans, egg and ½ cup of breadcrumbs into a separate mixing bowl. Transfer the onion mixture from the skillet into the bowl and stir all ingredients well.
5. Scoop the mixture and shape them into patties. Sprinkle the patties with the remaining breadcrumbs.
6. Set patties on a lightly greased baking sheet and broil in the broiler for 8-10 minutes. Turn over the patties then broil for another 8 – 10 minutes. The patties

should be cooked through and evenly browned.
7. Place the patties on hamburger buns and add mayonnaise before serving.

Red Pepper and Turkey Pasta

Ingredients:
- Large red bell peppers (3 pcs.)
- Extra virgin olive oil (3 tbsp.)
- Chopped large onion (1 pc.)
- Minced garlic (2 tsp.)
- Chopped oregano (2 tbsp.)
- Red wine vinegar (1 tbsp.)
- Ground turkey (2 lbs.) Cooked rigatoni (2 lbs.)

Instructions:
1. Cut bell pepper into halves, then remove the seeds and stem. Chop the peppers coarsely.
2. Heat oil in a pan over medium heat from a large Dutch oven. Add the onion and peppers into the pan and cook for 20 minutes or until the peppers are very tender.
3. Add garlic into the peppers and cook for five more minutes.

4. Transfer the onion-and-pepper mixture into a blender and puree until smooth. Transfer the mixture back to the saucepan and reheat over low to medium heat.
5. Add the vinegar and oregano. Stir well.
6. Sauté ground turkey in a separate skillet with little oil and cook until the turkey begins to brown. Add the turkey into the red pepper sauce, mix it well and let it simmer for 20 minutes.
7. Pour the pepper and turkey sauce over the cooked pasta then serve.

Weeknight Turkey Chili
Ingredients:
- Chopped large onion (1 pc.)
- Minced garlic (1 tbsp.)
- Ground turkey (1 ½ cups)
- Water (2 cups)
- Canned crushed tomatoes (1 28-oz. can)
- Drained kidney beans (1 16-oz. can)
- Chili powder (2 tbsp.)
- Turmeric (2 tsp.)
- Paprika (1 tsp.)

- Oregano (1 tsp.)
- Ground cumin (1 tsp.)
- Hot sauce (1 tsp.)

Instructions:

1. Cook onion in a large soup pot for 5 minutes, or until the onion starts to brown.
2. Add garlic and cook for 30 seconds.
3. Add ground turkey and stir continuously for 10 minutes until it is fully cooked.
4. Add water and all the remaining ingredients into the soup pot and bring to a boil.
5. Simmer with the pot uncovered for 30 – 45 minutes. Serve.

Brazil Nut-Crusted Tilapia with Sautéed Kale

Ingredients:

- Roasted Brazil nuts (1/4 cup)
- Bread crumbs (1/2 cup)
- Grated Parmesan cheese (2 tbsp.)
- Whole-grain mustard (1/4 cup)
- Tilapia fillets (1 ½ lbs.)
- Sesame oil (1 tbsp.)
- Mashed garlic (1 clove)

- Chopped kale (1 ½ heads)
- Kosher salt (1/4 tsp.)
- Toasted sesame seeds (2 tbsp.)

Instructions:

1. Preheat oven to 400'F.
2. Lightly grease a baking sheet. Set aside.
3. Add Brazil nuts in a food processor and pulse the nuts until they are finely ground. Transfer the nuts into a mixing bowl and add parmesan cheese and breadcrumbs. Stir the ingredients well.
4. Place tilapia fillets on the greased baking sheet and spread mustard on each fillet. Layer each fillet with the Brazil nut mixture.
5. Bake the tilapia fillets for 8 – 10 minutes or until the fish is thoroughly cooked.
6. In the meantime, heat a stainless-steel skillet over medium-high heat. Heat the sesame oil in the skillet for 15 seconds then add the garlic. Cook the garlic for 20 seconds then add kale. Stir the kale occasionally and cook for 7 -8 minutes.

7. Add sesame seeds into the skillet and toss the mixture until the kale is fully combined with the seeds.
8. Serve the fish fillets with a side of kale.

Poached Eggs with Curried Vegetables

Ingredients:
- Extra-virgin olive oil (2 tsp.)
- Chopped large onion (1 pc.)
- Minced garlic (1 clove)
- Yellow curry powder (1 tbsp.)
- Sliced button mushrooms (1/2 lb.)
- Diced zucchini (2 medium pcs.)
- Drained chickpeas (1 14-oz. can)
- Water (1 cup)
- White vinegar (1/2 tsp.)
- Large eggs (4 pcs.)
- Crushed red pepper (1/8 tsp.)

Instructions:
1. Sauté onion in a large non-stick skillet over medium to high heat for 4 -5 minutes, or until tender.
2. Add garlic and cook for 30 seconds. Add the curry powder and stir it well with the garlic and onion. Cook for another 1- 2 minutes.

3. Add mushrooms into the skillet and cook for another 5 minutes or until mushrooms become very tender.
4. Add chickpeas, red pepper, zucchini and water into the skillet and bring the mixture into a boil. Then let it simmer for 15 – 20 minutes or until zucchini is very tender.
5. In the meantime, add water in a separate saucepan to a depth of 3 inches. Boil the water, reduce heat, add vinegar and let it simmer.
6. Crack the eggs and slide each egg into the water one at a time, making sure it touches the surface of the water. Simmer the eggs for 3 -5 minutes, then remove the eggs with a large spoon.
7. Serve the eggs with a side of vegetables.

Quinoa & Turkey Stuffed Peppers
Ingredients:
- Uncooked quinoa (1 cup)
- Water (2 cups)
- Salt (½ tsp)

- Fully-cooked, diced smoked turkey sausage (½ pound)
- Chicken stock (½ cup)
- Extra-virgin olive oil (¼ cup)
- Chopped pecans, toasted (3 tbsp)
- Chopped fresh parsley (2 tbsp)
- Chopped fresh rosemary (2 tsp) Red bell peppers (3 pcs)

Instructions:

1. Using a large saucepan, stir the quinoa, salt, and water together. Boil the mixture in high-heat. Once boiling, reduce the heat and cover the saucepan. Simmer for about 15 minutes or until the water is almost completely absorbed.
2. Remove the cover and let the dish stand for 5 more minutes. Stir in the sausage together with the rest of the ingredients.
3. Fill the pepper with cooked quinoa mixture and put it on a slightly greased 13 x 9" baking dish. Bake the stuffed peppers for 15 minutes at 3500F heat.

Poached Black Sesame Salmon and Bok Choy Broth

Ingredients:

- Wild salmon (2 quarter pound pcs)
- Seafood stock (3 cups)
- Lime, thinly sliced (1 pc)
- Whole black peppercorns (10 pcs)
- Bok choy (2 heads)
- Lime juice (from 1 pc of lime)
- Salt and pepper, to taste
- Toasted black sesame seeds, for garnishing

Instructions:

1. In a heavy pot or deep skillet, mix the lime, peppercorn and seafood stock. Bring to a boil over high heat. Once boiling, lower the heat to a simmer immediately. Cover the pot and cook for another 5 minutes.

2. Season the salmon with salt & pepper, and then gently lower it to a simmering liquid. Be sure that the filets are ¾ covered (at the very least). Lower the heat to an even gentler simmer. Then cover the pot and cook for another 6 more minutes or until the salmon is

opaque all over (or when you are able to flake it using a fork). Take the salmon out of the liquid. Prepare a towel-lined plate and set the salmon on top.

3. Turn up the heat to medium setting to make the broth simmer at a steady pace. Toss in the bok choy heads and let them cook for around 3 minutes or until soft (not mushy so it would still result to a good bite). Remove the bok choy from the simmering liquid.

4. Turn up the heat once more, this time to medium high setting and continue cooking the broth for another 3 minutes. Put the lime juice in, then turn the heat off.

5. Halve the salmon and bok choy into two shallow bowls. Using a ladle, pour ¼ to ½ cup of broth on each bowl. Finish off by garnishing with black sesame seeds. Serve hot.

Almond Chicken

Ingredients
- Boneless chicken breast, sliced (3 oz.)

- Broccoli flowerets, steamed (2 cups)
- Olive oil (1 1/2 tsp)
- Green bell pepper, chopped (1 pc)
- Red bell pepper, chopped (1 pc)
- Onion, chopped (3/4 cup)
- Garlic, minced (1 clove)
- Cherry tomatoes, halved (1 cup)
- Salt & pepper, to taste
- Sliced almonds (2 tsp)

Instructions:

1. Steam the broccoli. At the same time, heat some olive oil in a saute pan.
2. Put the chicken, red and green pepper, garlic and onion in the pan and saute until the chicken is cooked inside and out, and the veggies are cooked al dente.
3. Toss in the steamed broccoli and tomatoes. Top with almonds.

Rice Pilaf

Ingredients:

- Olive oil (1 tsp)
- Finely chopped onion (2 tbsp.)
- Chicken broth (1 cup)
- Zone orzo (1/2 cup)

- Dried thyme (1/4 tsp) Salt & pepper to taste

Instructions:

1. Get a small saucepan and heat oil under medium heat setting. Add finely chopped onions. Cook until tender, stirring frequently.
2. Put a tablespoon of broth or as necessary.
3. Boil a cup of broth, then add Zone orzo. Stir until the broth is almost completely absorbed. That should take around 5 minutes.
4. Toss in the sautéed onion, salt & pepper, and thyme. Reduce heat and continue cooking until the broth is completely absorbed.
5. Gently fluff the rice with fork gently before serving.

Beef Barbecue withOnions

Ingredients:

- Olive oil, divided (1 1/2 tsp)
- Beef, eye of round (3 oz.)
- Tomato puree (1/2 cup)
- Worcestershire sauce (1 tsp)

- Cider vinegar (1/3 tsp)
- Chili powder (1/3 tsp)
- Cumin (1/8 tsp)
- Oregano (1/8 tsp)
- Onion, in half rings (1 cup)
- Garlic, minced (1 clove)
- Mushrooms (1 cup)
- Unsalted vegetable stock (2 tsp)
- White wine vinegar (2 tsp)
- Snow peas (1 cup)

Instructions:

1. Heat ½ tsp of oil in a skillet, then place the beef. Cook the beef until it is no longer pink
2. Add the Worcestershire sauce, puree, chili powder, cider vinegar, oregano, and cumin into the skillet.
3. Cover and allow to simmer for about 5 minutes or just until the sauce forms.
4. Get another skillet and put the remaining oil, garlic, and onion. Cook until the onion becomes tender.
5. Add garlic, onion, beef stock, white wine vinegar, and mushrooms to the beef. Cover the dish and allow to

cook for about 8 more minutes. Midway or after around 5 minutes, add the snow peas. Occasionally stir to blend the flavors well.

Citrus Tofu Salad

Ingredients

- Olive oil, divided (1 tsp)
- Worcestershire sauce (1/2 tsp)
- Celery salt (1/8 tsp)
- Extra firm tofu, ½" (6 oz.)
- Asparagus spears – 1" (1 1/2 cups)
- Celery, sliced (1 1/2 cups)
- Garlic, minced (1/2 tsp)
- Hot pepper sauce, dash (1/2 tsp)
- Paprika (1/2 tsp)
- Lemon herb seasoning (1/8 tsp)
- Dried dill (1/2 tsp)
- Salt & pepper, to taste
- Romaine lettuce (5 cups)
- Mandarin orange segments, in water (1/3 cup)

Instructions:

1. Get a medium-sized saute pan and spray with olive oil. Then, heat ½ tsp oil.

2. Blend the Worcestershire sauce, tofu, and celery salt in. Stir fry until all sides are crusted and browned.
3. Get another non-stick saute pan and heat the remaining oil. Stir fry the celery, asparagus, garlic, paprika, hot pepper sauce, dill, salt & pepper, and lemon herb seasoning until the veggies are crisp and tender.
4. Put some lettuce on a serving plate, with the orange segments evenly distributed over it.
5. To finish, top first with some veggie mixture, then finally with tofu.
6. Serve and enjoy!

American Chop Suey with Salad
Ingredients:
- Zone fusilli (2/3 cup)
- Olive oil (1 tsp)
- Celery, chopped (1/2 stalk)
- Onion, diced (3 tbsp.)
- Garlic, minced (1 clove)
- Red bell pepper, diced (3 tbsp.)

- Extra-lean turkey breast, ground (1 1/2 oz.)
- Cooking spray
- Canned tomatoes, diced (1/2 - 14.5 oz. can)
- Crushed red pepper flakes (1/4 tsp)
- Fresh chopped basil (1/4 tsp)
- Salt & pepper, to taste
- Freshly-squeezed lemon juice (1 tbsp.)
- Extra virgin olive oil (1 tsp)
- Lettuce (1/2 cup)
- Tomato (1/4 pc) Cucumber (1/4 pc)

Instructions:

1. Cook the Zone fusilli for 3 to 4 minutes. Set aside after draining.
2. Heat oil in a skillet under medium-high temperature setting. Toss in the onion and celery. Allow to cook for a few minutes before adding the peppers and garlic.
3. Remove the vegetables from the pan. Using a cooking spray, drizzle and saute the turkey until its color is no longer pinkish. Bring the vegetable mix back into the pan together with the partially cooked fusilli.

4. Top with crushed red pepper and canned tomatoes. Stir everything well before covering and allowing to simmer for another 8 minutes.
5. Top the dish with fresh basil right before serving, preferably with a small salad side.

Antipasto Salad

Ingredients:
- Iceberg lettuce, shredded (1 1/2 heads)
- Celery, sliced (2 cups)
- Carrots, sliced thin (3/4 cup)
- Mushrooms, sliced (3 cups)
- Onions, in half rings (1 cup)
- Red bell peppers, in half rings (2 1/4 cups)
- Garbanzo beans, canned (3/4 cup)
- Light tuna chunks, in water (2 oz.)
- Low-fat mozzarella cheese – shredded (2 oz.)
- Sliced turkey (3 oz.)
- Extra-lean ham slice (2 oz.)
- Dried basil - crushed in palm of hand (2 tsp)
- Extra virgin olive oil, drizzle (3 tsp)

- No-Fat Tasty Dressing - (1/4 cup)

Instructions:

1. Get 3 large-sized oval plates and set a lettuce bed on each one. Put the carrots, celery, mushrooms, red pepper, onions, and garbanzo beans on the bed of lettuce, forming a vertical line starting from the right side going to the left side of the plate.
2. Next, put the cheese, tuna, ham, and turkey on the plates, distributed evenly, using the strips of red bell pepper as divider.
3. Using your palm, crush the basil to release its freshness, and then sprinkle over the plates. Sprinkle a tsp of olive oil on all the plates. Whisk the dressing quickly before pouring on the salad.

Asian Stir Fried Chicken

Ingredients:

- Broccoli, chopped (3 cups)
- Olive oil (2 tsp)
- Skinless, boneless chicken breast (cut to bite sized pieces (7 oz.)
- Garlic, pressed (2 cloves)

- Water chestnuts, sliced (3/4 cup)
- Mushrooms, sliced (8 oz.)
- Red bell pepper, sliced (1 pc)
- Snow peas (1 cup)
- Scallions, sliced (1/2 cup)
- Low sodium soy sauce (2 tsp)
- Mandarin orange sections (1/2 cup)
- Toasted sesame oil (1 tsp)

Instructions:

1. Steam the broccoli for about 3 to 4 minutes. To stop cooking, rinse with some cold water. Set the broccoli aside and allow it to drain in a strainer.
2. Get a large-sized skillet and heat some olive oil under medium heat setting.
3. Add the garlic and chicken, and allow to cook until the juices are running clear. Then, add mushrooms, water chestnuts, scallions, snow peas, soy sauce, and pepper into the mix. Continue to cook until the veggies are tender. If necessary, add some vegetable stock in 1 tsp increments. Stir the sections of Mandarin orange in, together with the toasted sesame oil.
4. Transfer to a large plate and serve.

Printed in Great Britain
by Amazon